The Silly Little Book of KNOCK KNOCK JOKES

The Silly Little Book of

KNOCK KNOCK JOKES

p

This is a Parragon Book

This edition published in 2002

Parragon
Queen Street House
4 Queen Street
Bath BA1 1HE, UK

Produced by Magpie Books, an imprint of
Robinson Publishing Ltd, London

ISBN 0-75257-902-9

A copy of the British Library Cataloguing-in-Publication Data is available from the British Library

Printed and bound in Singapore

Contents

Introduction

Don't answer that door! It could be anyone out there, and you'll be in danger of splitting your sides with laughter when "Justine time" or "Amanda the table" comes calling. Check to see if there's a joke for your name and prepare for humor in the hallway and laughter through the letterbox as you leaf through this tremendous selection.

Girls' Names

Knock knock.

Who's there?

Ada.

Ada who?

Ada lot for breakfast.

Knock knock.
Who's there?
Amber.
Amber who?
Amberter than I was yesterday.

Knock knock.
Who's there?
Amy.
Amy who?
Amy for the top.

Knock knock.
Who's there?
Anna.
Anna who?
Annamazingly good joke.

Knock knock.
Who's there?
Annabel.
Annabel who?
Annabel would be useful on this door.

Knock knock.
Who's there?
Augusta.
Augusta who?
Augustalmost felt like winter.

Knock knock.
Who's there?
Aurora.
Aurora who?
Aurora's just come from a big lion!

Knock knock.

Who's there?

Ava.

Ava who?

Ava good mind to leave you.

Knock knock.

Who's there?

Barbara.

Barbara who?

(sing) "Barbara black sheep, have you any wool?"

Knock knock.

Who's there?

Barbie.

Barbie who?

Barbie Q.

Knock knock.

Who's there?

Bea.

Bea who?

Bea love and open the door.

Knock knock.
Who's there?
Bella.
Bella who?
Bella the ball.

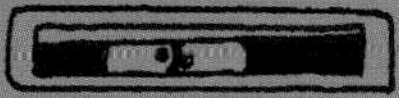

Knock knock.
Who's there?
Bernadette.
Bernadette who?
Bernadette my dinner.

Knock knock.

Who's there?

Beth.

Beth who?

Beth foot forward.

Knock knock.

Who's there?

Bethany.

Bethany who?

Bethany good shows recently?

Knock knock.

Who's there?

Bridie.

Bridie who?

Bridie light of the silvery moon.

Knock knock.

Who's there?

Caitlin.

Caitlin who?

Caitlin you my dress tonight – I'm wearing it.

Knock knock.
Who's there?
Camilla.
Camilla who?
Camilla minute!

Knock knock.
Who's there?
Candace.
Candace who?
Candace be love?

Knock knock.
Who's there?
Carmen.
Carmen who?
Carmen like best is a Ferrari.

Knock knock.
Who's there?
Carol.
Carol who?
Carol go if you switch the ignition on.

Knock knock.

Who's there?

Carrie.

Carrie who?

Carrie on with what you are doing.

Knock knock.

Who's there?

Cassie.

Cassie who?

Cassie you some time?

Knock knock.
Who's there?
Cecile.
Cecile who?
Cecile the envelope.

Knock knock.
Who's there?
Celeste.
Celeste who?
Celeste time I come calling.

Knock knock.
Who's there?
Cindy.
Cindy who?
Cindy parcel special delivery.

Knock knock.
Who's there?
Clara.
Clara who?
Clara space on the table.

Knock knock.
Who's there?
Colleen.
Colleen who?
Colleen yourself up, you're a mess!

Knock knock.
Who's there?
Courtney.
Courtney who?
Courtney robbers lately?

Knock knock.
Who's there?
Cynthia.
Cynthia who?
Cynthia won't listen, I'll keep shouting.

Knock knock.
Who's there?
Dana.
Dana who?
Dana you mind.

Knock knock.
Who's there?
Daryl.
Daryl who?
Daryl be the day.

Knock knock.

Who's there?

Dawn.

Dawn who?

Dawn do anything I wouldn't do.

Knock knock.

Who's there?

Della.

Della who?

Della tell ya that I love ya?

Knock knock.
Who's there?
Delphine.
Delphine who?
Delphine fine, thanks.

Knock knock.
Who's there?
Denise.
Denise who?
Denise are above de feet.

Knock knock.
Who's there?
Diana.
Diana who?
Diana thirst – a glass of water, please.

Knock knock.
Who's there?
Dolly.
Dolly who?
Dolly't them in, they're dangerous.

Knock knock.

Who's there?

Donna.

Donna who?

Donna you know? Isa Luigi.

Knock knock.

Who's there?

Dora.

Dora who?

Dora steel.

Knock knock.
Who's there?
Dorothy.
Dorothy who?
(*sing*) "Dorothynk I'm sexy?"

Knock knock.
Who's there?
Effie.
Effie who?
Effie'd known you were coming he'd have stayed home.

Knock knock.
Who's there?
Elizabeth.
Elizabeth who?
Elizabeth of knowledge is a dangerous thing.

Knock knock.
Who's there?
Ella.
Ella who?
Ella've good night!

Knock knock.

Who's there?

Ellen.

Ellen who?

Ellen high water.

Knock knock.

Who's there?

Miss Ellie.

Miss Ellie who?

Miss Ellie good shows lately?

Knock knock.
Who's there?
Elly.
Elly who?
Ellymentary, my dear Watson.

Knock knock.
Who's there?
Emma.
Emma who?
Emma new resident here - come round for tea.

Knock knock.

Who's there?

Enid.

Enid who?

Enid a glass of water.

Knock knock.

Who's there?

Erica.

Erica who?

Erica'd the last sweet.

Knock knock.
Who's there?
Erin.
Erin who?
Erin your lungs.

Knock knock.
Who's there?
Eunice.
Eunice who?
Eunice is like your nephew.

Knock knock.
Who's there?
Eva.
Eva who?
Eva had a smack in the mouth?

Knock knock.
Who's there?
Fanny.
Fanny who?
Fanny you not knowing who I am!

Knock knock.
Who's there?
Faye.
Faye who?
Fayeding away.

Knock knock.
Who's there?
Felicity.
Felicity who?
Felicity getting more polluted every day.

Knock knock.
Who's there?
Fifi.
Fifi who?
Fifiling c-cold, p-please l-let m-me in.

Knock knock.
Who's there?
Fiona.
Fiona who?
Fiona large house and a car.

Knock knock.
Who's there?
Fleur.
Fleur who?
Fleuride toothpaste.

Knock knock.

Who's there?

Flo.

Flo who?

Flo your candles out.

Knock knock.

Who's there?

Flora.

Flora who?

Florat the top of the block.

Knock knock.
Who's there?
Flossie.
Flossie who?
Flossie your teeth every day.

Knock knock.
Who's there?
Francoise.
Francoise who?
Francoise once a great empire.

Knock knock.

Who's there?

Gail.

Gail who?

Gail of laughter.

Knock knock.

Who's there?

Germaine.

Germaine who?

Germaine you don't recognize me?

Knock knock.

Who's there?

Gertie.

Gertie who?

Gertiesy call!

Knock knock.

Who's there?

Gilda.

Gilda who?

Gilda the picture frame.

Knock knock.
Who's there?
Giselle.
Giselle who?
Gisellegant and very pretty.

Knock knock.
Who's there?
Gita.
Gita who?
Gita job!

Knock knock.
Who's there?
Gladys.
Gladys who?
Gladys letter isn't a bill.

Knock knock.
Who's there?
Grace.
Grace who?
Grace skies are over us.

Knock knock.
Who's there?
Greta.
Greta who?
Greta job.

Knock knock.
Who's there?
Guinevere.
Guinevere who?
Guinevere going to get together?

Knock knock.
Who's there?
Hannah.
Hannah who?
Hannah cloth out to dry.

Knock knock.
Who's there?
Harriet.
Harriet who?
Harriet up!

Knock knock.
Who's there?
Hazel.
Hazel who?
Hazel restrict your vision.

Knock knock.
Who's there?
Heather.
Heather who?
Heather pothtman come yet?

Knock knock.
Who's there?
Hedda.
Hedda who?
Hedda ball in goal.

Knock knock.
Who's there?
Heidi.
Heidi who?
Heidi Clare war on you.

Knock knock.
Who's there?
Holly.
Holly who?
Hollylujah!

Knock knock.
Who's there?
Hope.
Hope who?
Hope you'll have me.

Knock knock.
Who's there?
Ida.
Ida who?
Ida bought a different knocker if I'd been you.

Knock knock.
Who's there?
Ida.
Ida who?
Ida know.

Knock knock.
Who's there?
Imogen.
Imogen who?
Imogenuine person.

Knock knock.
Who's there?
Ina.
Ina who?
Ina minute!

Knock knock.
Who's there?
Ina Claire.
Ina Claire who?
Ina Claire day you can see forever.

Knock knock.
Who's there?
Ina Minnie.
Ina Minnie who?
Ina Minnie miney mo.

Knock knock.
Who's there?
India.
India who?
India there's a bag belonging to me.

Knock knock.
Who's there?
Ines.
Ines who?
Inespecial place I'll hide your present.

Knock knock.
Who's there?
Ingrid.
Ingrid who?
Ingrid sorrow I have to leave you.

Knock knock.
Who's there?
Iona.
Iona who?
Iona house of my own, you know.

Knock knock.
Who's there?
Iris.
Iris who?
Iris you would open the door.

Knock knock.

Who's there?

Isabel.

Isabel who?

Isabel necessary on a bicycle?

Knock knock.

Who's there?

Isadore.

Isadore who?

Isadore on the right way round?

Knock knock.
Who's there?
Isla.
Isla who?
Isla be seeing you!

Knock knock.
Who's there?
Ivy.
Ivy who?
Ivyll cast a spell on you.

Knock knock.
Who's there?
Jackie.
Jackie who?
Jackie'n that job – it's killing you.

Knock knock.
Who's there?
Jacqueline.
Jacqueline who?
Jacqueline Hyde.

Knock knock.
Who's there?
Jade.
Jade who?
Jade a whole pie today.

Knock knock.
Who's there?
Jan.
Jan who?
Jan and bread.

Knock knock.
Who's there?
Janet.
Janet who?
Janet a big fish?

Knock knock.
Who's there?
Jasmine.
Jasmine who?
Jasmine like to play in bands.

Knock knock.
Who's there?
Jean.
Jean who?
Jeanius – you just don't recognize it.

Knock knock.
Who's there?
Jeanette.
Jeanette who?
Jeanette has too many holes in it, the fish will escape.

Knock knock.
Who's there?
Jenny.
Jenny who?
Jenny-d anything from the shops?

Knock knock.
Who's there?
Jessica.
Jessica who?
Jessica lot up last night?

Knock knock.
Who's there?
Joan.
Joan who?
Joan call us, we'll call you.

Knock knock.
Who's there?
Joanna.
Joanna who?
Joanna big kiss?

Knock knock.
Who's there?
Juanita.
Juanita who?
Juanita big meal?

Knock knock.
Who's there?
Judy.
Judy who?
Judy liver newspapers still?

Knock knock.
Who's there?
Julie.
Julie who?
Julie'n on this door a lot?

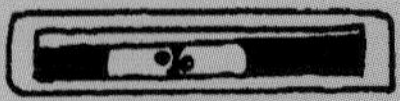

Knock knock.
Who's there?
Juliet.
Juliet who?
Juliet him get away with that?

Knock knock.
Who's there?
June.
June who?
June know how to open a door?

Knock knock.
Who's there?
Juno.
Juno who?
Juno how to get out of here?

Knock knock.
Who's there?
Justine.
Justine who?
Justine case.

Knock knock.
Who's there?
Katherine.
Katherine who?
Katherine together for a social evening.

Knock knock.
Who's there?
Kathy.
Kathy who?
Kathy you again?

Knock knock.

Who's there?

Kiki.

Kiki who?

Kiki's stuck in the lock – let me in.

Knock knock.

Who's there?

Kim.

Kim who?

Kim too late.

Knock knock.
Who's there?
Kristin.
Kristin who?
Kristining robe.

Knock knock.
Who's there?
Lacey.
Lacey who?
Lacey crazy days.

Knock knock.

Who's there?

Lana.

Lana who?

Lana the free.

Knock knock.

Who's there?

Lee.

Lee who?

Lee've it to me.

Knock knock.

Who's there?

Leonie.

Leonie who.

Leonie one I love.

Knock knock.

Who's there?

Leslie.

Leslie who?

Leslie town now before they catch us.

Knock knock.
Who's there?
Lucetta.
Lucetta who?
Lucetta a difficult problem.

Knock knock.
Who's there?
Lucille.
Lucille who?
Lucille ing is dangerous lo live under.

Knock knock.
Who's there?
Lucinda.
Lucinda who?
(sing) "Lucinda sky with diamonds . . ."

Knock knock.
Who's there?
Lucy.
Lucy who?
Lucylastic can let you down.

Knock knock.
Who's there?
Mae.
Mae who?
(sing) "Mae be it's because I'm a Londoner."

Knock knock.

Who's there?

Margo.

Margo who?

Margo, you're not needed now.

Knock knock.

Who's there?

Maria.

Maria who?

Marial name is Mary.

Knock knock.
Who's there?
Marian.
Marian who?
Mariand her little lamb.

Knock knock.
Who's there?
Marie.
Marie who?
Marie for love.

Knock knock.

Who's there?

Marietta.

Marietta who?

Marietta whole loaf!

Knock knock.

Who's there?

Marilyn.

Marilyn who?

Marilyn, she'll make you a good wife.

Knock knock.
Who's there?
Marion.
Marion who?
Marion idiot and repent at leisure.

Knock knock.
Who's there?
Martha.
Martha who?
Martha boys next door are hurting me!

Knock knock.
Who's there?
Mary.
Mary who?
That's what I keep wondering.

Knock knock.
Who's there?
Maude.
Maude who?
Mauden my job's worth.

Knock knock.
Who's there?
Mavis.
Mavis who?
Mavis be the best day of your life.

Knock knock.
Who's there?
Maxine.
Maxine who?
Maxine a lot of things.

Knock knock.
Who's there?
May.
May who?
Maybe it's a friend at the door.

Knock knock.
Who's there?
Maya.
Maya who?
Maya turn.

Knock knock.

Who's there?

Meg.

Meg who?

Meg a fuss.

Knock knock.

Who's there?

Megan.

Megan who?

Megan a loud noise.

Knock knock.
Who's there?
Michelle.
Michelle who?
Michelle has sounds of the sea
in it.

Knock knock.
Who's there?
Mimi.
Mimi who?
Mimi b-bicycle's b-broken.

Knock knock.
Who's there?
Minnie.
Minnie who?
Minnie people want to come in.

Knock knock.
Who's there?
Miranda.
Miranda who?
Miranda friend want to come in.

Knock knock.

Who's there.

Nadia.

Nadia who?

Nadia head if you want to come in.

Knock knock.

Who's there?

Nancy.

Nancy who?

Nancy a piece of cake?

Knock knock.
Who's there?
Nicky.
Nicky who?
Nicky nacks.

Knock knock.
Who's there?
Nola.
Nola who?
Nolaner driver may drive a car alone.

Knock knock.
Who's there?
Norma.
Norma who?
Normally the butler opens the door.

Knock knock.
Who's there?
Olga.
Olga who?
Olga home now.

Knock knock.
Who's there?
Olive.
Olive who?
Olive in this house – what are you doing there?

Knock knock.

Who's there?

Olivia.

Olivia who?

Olivia'l is great for cooking.

Knock knock.

Who's there?

Onya.

Onya who?

Onya marks, get set, go.

Knock knock.
Who's there?
Pam.
Pam who?
Pamper yourself.

Knock knock.
Who's there?
Pammy.
Pammy who?
Pammy something nice when you are at the shops!

Knock knock.
Who's there?
Patty.
Patty who?
Patty-cake.

Knock knock.
Who's there?
Peg.
Peg who?
Peg your pardon, I've got the wrong door.

Knock knock.
Who's there?
Penny.
Penny who?
Penny for your thoughts.

Knock knock.
Who's there?
Petal.
Petal who?
Petal fast, we're nearly there.

Knock knock.
Who's there?
Phoebe.
Phoebe who?
Phoebe way above my price.

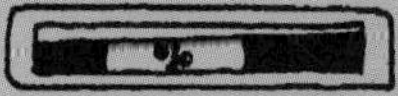

Knock knock.
Who's there?
Phyllis.
Phyllis who?
Phyllis up.

Knock knock.
Who's there?
Polly.
Polly who?
Polly the other one, it's got bells on.

Knock knock.
Who's there?
Poppy.
Poppy who?
Poppy'n any time you like.

Knock knock.
Who's there?
Portia.
Portia who?
Portia the door – it's stuck.

Knock knock.
Who's there?
Rena.
Rena who?
Renamok in the shopping mall.

Knock knock.
Who's there?
Renata.
Renata who?
Renata sugar. Can I borrow some?

Knock knock.
Who's there?
Rhona.
Rhona who?
Rhonaround town.

Knock knock.

Who's there?

Rhonda.

Rhonda who?

Rhonda why?

Knock knock.

Who's there?

Rita.

Rita who?

Rita novel.

Knock knock.
Who's there?
Rose.
Rose who?
Rose early one morning.

Knock knock.
Who's there?
Rosina.
Rosina who?
Rosina vase.

Knock knock.
Who's there?
Ruth.
Ruth who?
Ruthless people.

Knock knock.
Who's there?
Saffron.
Saffron who?
Saffron a chair and it collapsed.

Knock knock.
Who's there?
Sally.
Sally who?
Sallyeverything you've got.

Knock knock.
Who's there?
Samantha.
Samantha who?
Samantha baby have gone for a walk.

Knock knock.
Who's there?
Sandra.
Sandra who?
Sandrabout your toes on the beach.

Knock knock.
Who's there?
Sandy.
Sandy who?
Sandy shore.

Knock knock.
Who's there?
Sarah.
Sarah who?
Sarah doctor in the house?

Knock knock.
Who's there?
Serena.
Serena who?
Serena round the corner.

Knock knock.
Who's there?
Sharon.
Sharon who?
Sharon share alike – would you like some of my chocolate?

Knock knock.
Who's there?
Shelby.
Shelby who?
(*sing*) "Shelby coming round the mountain when she comes."

Knock knock.
Who's there?
Sherry.
Sherry who?
Sherry trifle!

Knock knock.
Who's there?
Shirley.
Shirley who?
Shirley you know who I am!

Knock knock.
Who's there?
Sonia.
Sonia who?
Sonia shoe – it's stinking the house out.

Knock knock.
Who's there?
Stacey.
Stacey who?
Stacey what happens next.

Knock knock.
Who's there?
Stella.
Stella who?
Stella lot from the rich people.

Knock knock.
Who's there?
Stephanie.
Stephanie who?
Stephanie gas – we need to go faster!

Knock knock.
Who's there?
Sue.
Sue who?
Sue'n you will know.

Knock knock.
Who's there?
Sybil.
Sybil who?
Sybiling rivalry.

Knock knock.
Who's there?
Tamsin.
Tamsin who?
Tamsin time again I come to the wrong house.

Knock knock.
Who's there?
Tania.
Tania who?
Tania self round, you'll see.

Knock knock.
Who's there?
Tara.
Tara who?
Tararaboomdeay.

Knock knock.
Who's there?
Tiffany.
Tiffany who?
Tiffany rubbish out of the bag
before you use it.

Knock knock.
Who's there?
Tilly.
Tilly who?
Tilly cows come home.

Knock knock.
Who's there?
Tina.
Tina who?
Tina tomatoes.

Knock knock.

Who's there?

Tori.

Tori who?

Tori I upset you.

Knock knock.

Who's there?

Tracy.

Tracy who?

Tracy the shape in pencil.

Knock knock.
Who's there?
Tricia.
Tricia who?
Bless you – what a bad cold!

Knock knock.
Who's there?
Trudy.
Trudy who?
Trudy your word.

Knock knock.

Who's there?

Una.

Una who?

Yes, Una who.

Knock knock.

Who's there?

Utica.

Utica who?

(*sing*) "Utica high road and I'll take the low road."

Knock knock.
Who's there?
Vanda.
Vanda who?
Vanda you vant me to come round?

Knock knock.
Who's there?
Vanessa.
Vanessa who?
Vanessa time I'll ring the bell.

Knock knock.

Who's there?

Viola.

Viola who?

Viola sudden you don't know who I am?

Knock knock.

Who's there?

Violet.

Violet who?

Violet the cat out of the bag.

Knock knock.
Who's there?
Wendy.
Wendy who?
Wendy come to take you away
I won't stop them!

Knock knock.
Who's there?
Willa.
Willa who?
Willa present make you happy?

Knock knock.
Who's there?
Winnie.
Winnie who?
Winnie is better than losing.

Knock knock.
Who's there?
Xena.
Xena who?
Xena minute!

Knock knock.
Who's there?
Yvette.
Yvette who?
Yvette helps lots of animals.

Knock knock.
Who's there?
Yvonne.
Yvonne who?
Yvonne to know vat you are doing.

Knock knock.

Who's there?

Zoe.

Zoe who?

Zoe said that, did he? Don't believe him.

Boys' Names

Knock knock.
Who's there?
Aaron.
Aaron who?
Aaron the chest means strength in arms.

Knock knock.
Who's there?
Abel.
Abel who?
Abel to go to work.

Knock knock.
Who's there?
Adair.
Adair who?
Adair you to open this door.

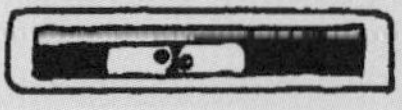

Knock knock.
Who's there?
Adam.
Adam who?
Adam nuisance come to borrow some sugar.

Knock knock.

Who's there?

Al.

Al who?

Al be seeing you!

Knock knock.

Who's there?

Alan.

Alan who?

Alan a good cause.

Knock knock.
Who's there?
Albert.
Albert who?
Albert you'll never guess.

Knock knock.
Who's there?
Aldo.
Aldo who?
Aldo the washing up tonight.

Knock knock.
Who's there?
Alec.
Alec who?
Alec your sister but I don't like you.

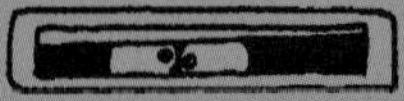

Knock knock.
Who's there?
Alex.
Alex who?
Alex plain later if you let me in.

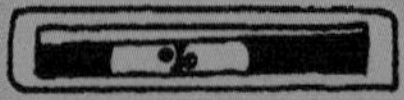

Knock knock.
Who's there?
Alexander.
Alexander who?
Alexander friend want to come over.

Knock knock.
Who's there?
Alf.
Alf who?
Alf way home.

Knock knock.
Who's there?
Alfie.
Alfie who?
Alfie terrible if you leave.

Knock knock.

Who's there?

Alistair.

Alistair who?

Alistairs in this house are broken.

Knock knock.

Who's there?

Alvin.

Alvin who?

Alvin zis competition – Just vait and see!

Knock knock.

Who's there?

Amos.

Amos who?

Amos be mad! This isn't my house.

Knock knock.

Who's there?

Andrew.

Andrew who?

Andrew a picture on the wall.

Knock knock.

Who's there?

Barry.

Barry who?

Barry the dead.

Knock knock.

Who's there?

Ben.

Ben who?

Ben down and tie your shoelaces.

Knock knock.

Who's there?

Benjamin.

Benjamin who.

Benjamin the blues.

Knock knock.

Who's there?

Bernie.

Bernie who?

Bernie bridges.

Knock knock.
Who's there?
Bert.
Bert who?
Bert the cakes.

Knock knock.
Who's there?
Bill.
Bill who?
Bill of rights.

Knock knock.
Who's there?
Bjorn.
Bjorn who?
Bjorn free.

Knock knock.

Who's there?

Bruno.

Bruno who?

Bruno more tea for me.

Knock knock.

Who's there?

Buster.

Buster who?

Buster the town, please.

Knock knock.

Who's there?

Caesar.

Caesar who?

Caesar jolly good fellow.

Knock knock.

Who's there?

Cain.

Cain who?

Cain tell you.

Knock knock.
Who's there?
Callum.
Callum who?
Callum all back.

Knock knock.
Who's there?
Carl.
Carl who?
Carl you see?

Knock knock.
Who's there?
Charles.
Charles who?
Charles your luck on the roulette wheel.

Knock knock.

Who's there?

Chester.

Chester who?

Chester minute! Don't you know who I am?

Knock knock.

Who's there?

Chris.

Chris who?

Chrismas stocking.

Knock knock.

Who's there?

Chuck.

Chuck who?

Chuck in a sandwich for lunch!

Knock knock.

Who's there?

Cliff.

Cliff who?

Cliffhanger.

Knock knock.

Who's there?

Cohen.

Cohen who?

Cohen your way.

Knock knock.

Who's there?

Colin.

Colin who?

Colin all cars . . . Colin all cars . . .

Knock knock.

Who's there?

Cosmo.

Cosmo who?

Cosmo trouble than you're worth.

Knock knock.

Who's there?

Costas.

Costas who?

Costas a fortune to get here.

Knock knock.
Who's there?
Craig.
Craig who?
Craig in the wall.

Knock knock.
Who's there?
Crispin.
Crispin who?
Crispin crunchy is how I like my cereal.

Knock knock.

Who's there?

Cyril.

Cyril who?

Cyril animals at the zoo.

Knock knock.

Who's there?

Dale.

Dale who?

Dale come if you call dem.

Knock knock.
Who's there?
Danny.
Danny who?
Dannybody home?

Knock knock.
Who's there?
Darren.
Darren who?
Darren the garden, hiding.

Knock knock.

Who's there?

Dave.

Dave who?

Dave of glory.

Knock knock.

Who's there?

Derek.

Derek who?

Derek get richer and the poor get poorer.

Knock knock.

Who's there?

Desi.

Desi who?

Desi take sugar?

Knock knock.

Who's there?

Devlin.

Devlin who?

Devlin a red dress.

Knock knock.
Who's there?
Dewey.
Dewey who?
Dewey stay or do we go now?

Knock knock.
Who's there?
Diego.
Diego who?
Diego before de "B".

Knock knock.

Who's there?

Don.

Don who?

Don take me for granted.

Knock knock.

Who's there?

Douglas.

Douglas who?

Douglas is broken.

Knock knock.

Who's there?

Duane.

Duane who?

Duane gonna get away with dis!

Knock knock.

Who's there?

Duncan.

Duncan who?

Duncan biscuit in your tea.

Knock knock.

Who's there?

Dwight.

Dwight who?

Dwight house is where the president lives.

Knock knock.
Who's there?
Edwin.
Edwin who?
Edwin a cup if I could run faster.

Knock knock.
Who's there?
Egbert.
Egbert who?
Egbert no bacon.

Knock knock.

Who's there?

Eli.

Eli who?

Eli, eli, oh!

Knock knock.

Who's there?

Ellis.

Ellis who?

Ellis damnation.

Knock knock.
Who's there?
Emil.
Emil who?
Emil would be nice if you've got some food.

Knock knock.
Who's there?
Emmett.
Emmett who?
Emmett the front door, not the back.

Knock knock.
Who's there?
Ethan.
Ethan who?
Ethan all my dinner.

Knock knock.
Who's there?
Eugene.
Eugene who?
Eugene, me Tarzan.

Knock knock.

Who's there?

Evan.

Evan who?

Evan only knows!

Knock knock.

Who's there?

Ewan.

Ewan who?

Ewan me should get together.

Knock knock.

Who's there?

Ezra.

Ezra who?

Ezra room to rent?

Knock knock.

Who's there?

Felix.

Felix who?

Felixtremely cold.

Knock knock.
Who's there?
Fido.
Fido who?
Fido known you were coming I'd have baked a cake.

Knock knock.
Who's there?
Fletcher.
Fletcher who?
Fletcher stick, there's a good boy.

Knock knock.

Who's there?

Foster.

Foster who?

Foster than a speeding bullet.

Knock knock.

Who's there?

Francis.

Francis who?

Francis where the French live.

Knock knock.

Who's there?

Frank.

Frank who?

Frank you very much.

Knock knock.

Who's there?

Franz.

Franz who?

Franz, Romans, countrymen, lend me your ears.

Knock knock.

Who's there?

Fred.

Fred who?

Fred this needle – I'm cross-eyed.

Knock knock.
Who's there?
Freddie.
Freddie who?
Freddie won't come out to play today.

Knock knock.
Who's there?
Gary.
Gary who?
Gary on smiling.

Knock knock.
Who's there?
Geoff.
Geoff who?
Geoff feel like going out tonight?

Knock knock.
Who's there?
Giuseppe.
Giuseppe who?
Giuseppe credit cards?

Knock knock.
Who's there?
Grant.
Grant who?
Grant three wishes.

Knock knock.
Who's there?
Greg.
Greg who?
Greg Scott!

Knock knock.
Who's there?
Gus.
Gus who?
Gus what – it's me!

Knock knock.
Who's there?
Guthrie.
Guthrie who?
Guthrie ice-creams in my hand.

Knock knock.
Who's there?
Hank.
Hank who?
Hank you for asking.

Knock knock.
Who's there?
Hans.
Hans who?
Hans across the sea.

Knock knock.
Who's there?
Harry.
Harry who?
Harry up!

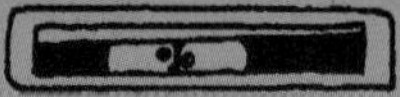

Knock knock.
Who's there?
Hayden.
Hayden who?
Hayden behind the door.

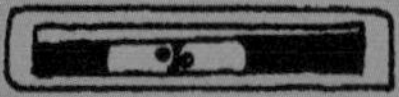

Knock knock.
Who's there?
Herman.
Herman who?
Herman dry.

Knock knock.
Who's there?
Hiram.
Hiram who?
Hiram and fire 'em.

Knock knock.
Who's there?
Horatio.
Horatio who?
Horatio to the end of the road.

Knock knock.
Who's there?
Howard.
Howard who?
Howard you know? You won't even open up.

Knock knock.
Who's there?
Howie.
Howie who?
Fine thanks. How are you?

Knock knock.
Who's there?
Huey.
Huey who?
Who am I? I'm me!

Knock knock.
Who's there?
Hugh.
Hugh who?
Hugh wouldn't believe it if I told you.

Knock knock.
Who's there?
Ian.
Ian who?
Ian a lot of money.

Knock knock.

Who's there?

Ike.

Ike who?

Ike'n see you through the keyhole.

Knock knock.

Who's there?

Ira.

Ira who?

Irate – or I will be if I stand out here any longer!

Knock knock.
Who's there?
Isaac.
Isaac who?
Isaac all my staff today.

Knock knock.
Who's there?
Ivan.
Ivan who?
Ivan enormous snake in my pocket.

Knock knock.
Who's there?
Ivor.
Ivor who?
Ivor lot more jokes where this came from!

Knock knock.
Who's there?
Jack.
Jack who?
Jack in the box.

Knock knock.
Who's there?
James.
James who?
James people play.

Knock knock.
Who's there?
Jamie.
Jamie who?
Jamie'n you don't recognize my voice?

Knock knock.
Who's there?
Jason.
Jason who?
Jason a rainbow.

Knock knock.
Who's there?
Jay.
Jay who?
Jay what you mean.

Knock knock.
Who's there?
Jeff.
Jeff who?
Jeff fancy going out tonight?

Knock knock.
Who's there?
Jeffrey.
Jeffrey who?
Jeffrey time I knock, you ask who I am.

Knock knock.
Who's there?
Jerome.
Jerome who?
Jerome alone.

Knock knock.
Who's there?
Jerry.
Jerry who?
Jerry cake.

Knock knock.
Who's there?
Jess.
Jess who?
Don't know, you tell me.

Knock knock.
Who's there?
Jesse.
Jesse who?
Jesse if you can recognize my voice.

Knock knock.
Who's there?
Jethro.
Jethro who?
Jethro our ball back, please?

Knock knock.
Who's there?
Jim.
Jim who?
Jim mind if we come and stay with you?

Knock knock.
Who's there?
Jimmy.
Jimmy who?
Jimmy all your money.

Knock knock.
Who's there?
Joe.
Joe who?
Joe away – I'm not talking to you.

Knock knock.
Who's there?
Johann.
Johann who?
Johann! How you doing, dude!

Knock knock.
Who's there?
John.
John who?
John in the fun.

Knock knock.
Who's there?
Juan.
Juan who?
Just Juan of those things.

Knock knock.
Who's there?
Jude.
Jude who?
Jude doubt me? Just open up.

Knock knock.
Who's there?
Julian.
Julian who?
Juliand I are going shopping now.

Knock knock.
Who's there?
Justin.
Justin who?
Justin time.

Knock knock.
Who's there?
Keith.
Keith who?
Keith your hands off me!

Knock knock.
Who's there?
Ken.
Ken who?
Ken you come and play?

Knock knock.
Who's there?
Kenneth.
Kenneth who?
Kenneth three little kittens come out to play?

Knock knock.

Who's there?

Kevin.

Kevin who?

Kevin and sit down.

Knock knock.

Who's there?

Kurt.

Kurt who?

Kurt and wounded.

Knock knock.
Who's there?
Kyle.
Kyle who?
Kyle be good if you let me in!

Knock knock.
Who's there?
Larry.
Larry who?
Larry up.

Knock knock.

Who's there?

Laurie.

Laurie who?

Laurie-load of goods.

Knock knock.

Who's there?

Len.

Len who?

Len us a fiver will you?

Knock knock.
Who's there?
Leon.
Leon who?
Leon me – I'll support you.

Knock knock.
Who's there?
Les.
Les who?
Les see what we can do.

Knock knock.
Who's there?
Lester.
Lester who?
Lester we forget.

Knock knock.
Who's there?
Lewis.
Lewis who?
Lewis all my money in a poker game.

Knock knock.
Who's there?
Lionel.
Lionel who?
Lionel roar if you stand on its tail.

Knock knock.
Who's there?
Lloyd.
Lloyd who?
Lloyd him away with an ice-cream.

Knock knock.
Who's there?
Lou.
Lou who?
Lou's your money on the horses.

Knock knock.
Who's there?
Luke.
Luke who?
Luke through the peep-hole and you'll see.

Knock knock.
Who's there?
Luther.
Luther who?
Luther please – not tho tight!

Knock knock.
Who's there?
Lyle.
Lyle who?
Lyle low until the cops have gone.

Knock knock.
Who's there?
Malcolm.
Malcolm who?
Malcolm outside and play!

Knock knock.
Who's there?
Marcus.
Marcus who?
Marcus a really nice boy.

Knock knock.
Who's there?
Mark.
Mark who?
Mark my words.

Knock knock.
Who's there?
Marvin.
Marvin who?
Marvin at these amazing tricks.

Knock knock.
Who's there?
Mel.
Mel who?
Melt down!

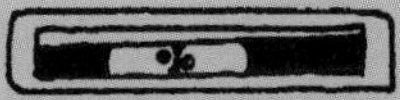

Knock knock.
Who's there?
Michael.
Michael who?
Michaelock has stopped ticking.

Knock knock.
Who's there?
Mike.
Mike who?
Mike the best of it.

Knock knock.
Who's there?
Mikey.
Mikey who?
Mikey is stuck.

Knock knock.
Who's there?
Miles.
Miles who?
Miles away.

Knock knock.

Who's there?

Milo.

Milo who?

Milo bed is too uncomfortable.

Knock knock.

Who's there?

Misha.

Misha who?

Misha lot of things while I was away?

Knock knock.
Who's there?
Murphy.
Murphy who?
Murphy, murphy me!

Knock knock.
Who's there?
Murray.
Murray who?
Murray me now.

Knock knock.

Who's there?

Neil.

Neil who?

Neil down and pray.

Knock knock.

Who's there?

Nicholas.

Nicholas who?

Nicholas girls shouldn't climb trees.

Knock knock.
Who's there?
Nick.
Nick who?
Nick R. Elastic.

Knock knock.
Who's there?
Noah.
Noah who?
Noah don't know who you are either.

Knock knock.

Who's there?

Norman.

Norman who?

Norman behavior is expected here.

Knock knock.

Who's there?

Oliver.

Oliver who?

Oliver long way away.

Knock knock.
Who's there?
Omar.
Omar who?
Omar goodness, what are you doing in there?

Knock knock.
Who's there?
Oscar.
Oscar who?
Oscar a foolish question, get a foolish answer.

Knock knock.
Who's there?
Othello.
Othello who?
Othello I wouldn't trust an inch.

Knock knock.
Who's there?
Owen.
Owen who?
Owen up, we all know you did it.

Knock knock.
Who's there?
Pablo.
Pablo who?
Pablo the candles out.

Knock knock.
Who's there?
Patrick.
Patrick who?
Patricked me into coming.

Knock knock.
Who's there?
Paul.
Paul who?
Paul up a chair and I'll tell you.

Knock knock.
Who's there?
Percy.
Percy who?
Percy Verence is the secret of success.

Knock knock.
Who's there?
Perry.
Perry who?
Perry well, thank you.

Knock knock.
Who's there?
Philip.
Philip who?
Philip the car with petrol.

Knock knock.
Who's there?
Pierre.
Pierre who?
Pierre through the keyhole – you'll see.

Knock knock.
Who's there?
Ray.
Ray who?
Ray drops keep falling on my head.

Knock knock.
Who's there?
Raymond.
Raymond who?
Raymond me to take that book back.

Knock knock.
Who's there?
Reuben.
Reuben who?
Reuben my eyes.

Knock knock.
Who's there?
Richard.
Richard who?
Richard poor have little in common.

Knock knock.
Who's there?
Robert.
Robert who?
Roberts are taking over the world.

Knock knock.
Who's there?
Robin.
Robin who?
Robin banks.

Knock knock.

Who's there?

Roland.

Roland who?

Roland butter please.

Knock knock.

Who's there?

Romeo.

Romeo who?

Romeover the river.

Knock knock.
Who's there?
Ron.
Ron who?
Ron way round.

Knock knock.
Who's there?
Rudi.
Rudi who?
Rudi toot!

Knock knock.
Who's there?
Russell.
Russell who?
Russelling leaves.

Knock knock.
Who's there?
Sam.
Sam who?
Sam day you'll recognize my voice.

Knock knock.
Who's there?
Saul.
Saul who?
Saul I know.

Knock knock.
Who's there?
Scott.
Scott who?
Scott nothing to do with you.

Knock knock.

Who's there?

Sebastian.

Sebastian who?

Sebastian of society.

Knock knock.

Who's there?

Seymour.

Seymour who?

Seymour from the top window.

Knock knock.
Who's there?
Sid.
Sid who?
Sid on it!

Knock knock.
Who's there?
Simon.
Simon who?
Simon time again I've told you not to do that.

Knock knock.
Who's there?
Sonny.
Sonny who?
Sonny outside, isn't it?

Knock knock.
Who's there?
Stan.
Stan who?
Stan back, I'm going to be sick.

Knock knock.
Who's there?
Stefan.
Stefan who?
Stefan it!

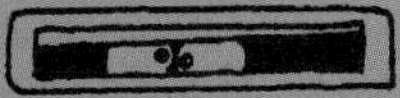

Knock knock.

Who's there?

Steve.

Steve who?

Steve upper lip.

Knock knock.

Who's there?

Stevie.

Stevie who.

Stevie has terrible reception.

Knock knock.

Who's there?

Talbot.

Talbot who?

Talbot too thin.

Knock knock.

Who's there?

Theodore.

Theodore who?

Theodore is locked.

Knock knock.
Who's there?
Thomas.
Thomas who?
Thomaster a language takes a long time.

Knock knock.
Who's there?
Tim.
Tim who?
Tim after time.

Knock knock.
Who's there?
Toby.
Toby who?
Toby or not Toby, that is the question.

Knock knock.
Who's there?
Tommy.
Tommy who?
Tommy you will always be beautiful.

Knock knock.
Who's there?
Tristan.
Tristan who?
Tristan elephant not to forget.

Knock knock.
Who's there?
Troy.
Troy who?
Troy the bell instead.

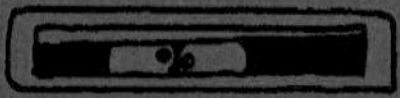

Knock knock.

Who's there?

Vic.

Vic who?

Victory parade.

Knock knock.
Who's there?
Vincent.
Vincent who?
Vincent me here.

Knock knock.
Who's there?
Wade.
Wade who?
Wading room.

Knock knock.
Who's there?
Walter.
Walter who?
Walter, walter everywhere and not a drop to drink.

Knock knock.
Who's there?
Wayne.
Wayne who?
(*sing*) "Wayne in a manger, no crib for a bed."

Knock knock.
Who's there?
Wesley.
Wesley who?
Wesley wind is blowing out here.

Knock knock.
Who's there?
Will.
Will who?
Will you go away?

Knock knock.
Who's there?
Woody.
Woody who?
Woody come if we asked him?

Knock knock.
Who's there?
Xavier.
Xavier who?
Xavier breath! I'm not leaving.

Knock knock.
Who's there?
York.
York who?
York, york, york. This is funny.

Knock knock.
Who's there?
Yul.
Yul who?
Yuletide.